Why Otters Don't Wear Socks

Roger Stevens used to live in a big city, but moved to a cottage in the country so that he could look out for sock-less otters, frock-less frogs and boot-less bumblebees. When he is not writing poems he visits schools, festivals and libraries, performing poetry and music and making people laugh. He has written several novels for children and hundreds of poems, which you can find in lots of anthologies. This is his third solo poetry collection for Macmillan. Visit his award-winning website at www.poetryzone.co.uk

Sarah Nayler was born in Southend-on-Sea. She has illustrated numerous books of poetry and children's fiction, including the work of Kez Grey, Jenny Oldfield and Dick King-Smith. She has also won critical acclaim for her own as-yet unpublished children's stories from husband Tim, children Alfie and Polly, and Daisy the Jack Russell (not to mention the cat, Stinky Tinky), with whom she lives a happily chaotic life in Hertfordshire.

Also published by Macmillan Children's Books

The Monster that Ate the Universe
Poems by Roger Stevens

How to Survive School
Poems chosen by David Harmer

Can We Have Our Ball Back, Please?
Football poems by Gareth Owen

Silly Superstitions
Poems chosen by Graham Denton

Why Otters Don't Wear Socks

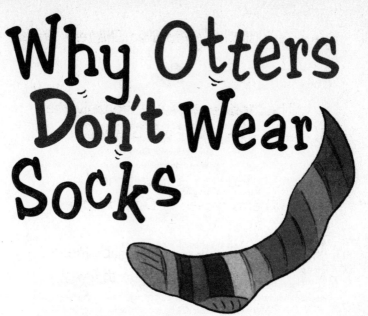

Poems by
Roger Stevens

Illustrated
by Sarah Nayler

MACMILLAN CHILDREN'S BOOKS

For Lily, Ruby and Merlin

First published 2007 by Macmillan Children's Books
a division of Macmillan Publishers Limited
20 New Wharf Road, London N1 9RR
Basingstoke and Oxford
www.panmacmillan.com

Associated companies throughout the world

ISBN: 978-0-330-44851-2

1 3 5 7 9 8 6 4 2

A CIP catalogue record for this book is available from
the British Library.

Typeset by Tony Fleetwood
Printed and bound in Great Britain by Mackays of Chatham plc, Kent

Visit **www.panmacmillan.com** to read more about all our books and to buy
them. You will also find features, author interviews and news of any author
events, and you can sign up for e-newsletters so that you're always first to hear
about our new releases.

Contents

It's a Tough Life   1

A Happy Poem and a Sad Poem   2

What's My Name?   4

Sadness   6

The Millennium Falcon   8

Making a Poem   9

Half Rhymes   10

Wind Haiku   11

Commas   12

Change of Position   14

Alone in the Classroom   17

Bad Speller's Acrostic   18

Who Lives in the School Pond?   19

The Water Cycle   20

More Commas   22

Silent Song   23

Penalty Shot   24

Why Me?   26

Travelling   27

Mirror Image   28

Holiday in Provence   30

Italian Poem   32

Old Salt   34

Death Cycle Haiku   36

Farewell, Pete   37

My Mobile Phone   38

What a Racket   40

Earthquake   42

Photograph   43

Whoops!   44

The Owl and the Pussycat   45

Hey Diddle Diddle   46

Peter Piper   48

Kubla Khant   49

Oak   50

October   52

The Things a Dog Has to Do   53

Mirror Haiku   56

Hammy Hamster's Great Adventure   58

Stone   60

Cold Spell   61

Crow Haiku   62

The Brown Bear   63

The Ghostly Visitor   65

A Poem's Plea   68

Nineteen Things to Do in Winter   70

Protection   72

She is   73

Liverpool Cathedral   74

Christmas Morning   76

Frequently Asked Questions   79

Mum's Grave   81

What's the Point?   82

Freedom   83

It's a Tough Life

It's tough being a poet
Up at the crack of midday
Thinking of rhyme schemes and rhythms
Trying to think what to say

It's tough being a poet
Strolling along the beach
Searching for inspiration
When inspiration's a wave out of reach

I sometimes think that a poet
Is the toughest thing you can be
As I walk in the shade of the forest
Trying to think of a rhyme for tree

A Happy Poem
and a Sad Poem

Hugs
Apples
Playtime
Pets
Yellow

jes**S**
dropped her pizz**A**
and crie**D**

3

What's My Name?

I'm the sun that lights the playground before the work begins
I'm the smile when teacher cracks a joke
I'm the giggles and the grins
In assembly I'm the trophy that the winning team collects
In your maths book I'm the page of sums where
     every one's correct
I'm the pure blue sky and leafy green that wins the prize
    in art
I'm steamy, creamy custard dribbling down the
    cook's jam tart
I'm the noise of playtime rising through the stratosphere
I'm the act of kindness when you lent your kit to Mia
I'm the star you were awarded for your startling poetry
I'm the school gates swinging open on the stroke of
    half past three
If you look for me, you'll find me
What's my name?
Can you guess?
I live just round the corner and my name is happiness

Sadness

I am the click of the catch
The heavy clunk
Of the closing door

The final words that hang in the air

The precious seconds of stillness

Before your mother starts crying
Before she grabs your hand
Before the carriage jerks and moves
Before your father half smiles at you, half waves

And the train leaves the station forever

The Millennium Falcon

Okay
I know
You're right
It doesn't look much
A plastic tube
Metallic paint, some wood, some wire
But it's the Millennium Falcon
Spaceship for hire

It's been travelling the universe
For five years and a day
And it was built by grandad
Before he passed away

Okay
I know
You're right
It doesn't look much
Metallic paint, some wire, some wood
But it fought and beat the Empire
For the forces of good

And now, upon my bedroom shelf
It's found its final rest
I know it doesn't look much
But in its day it was the best

Making a Poem

If you say
something
and make it rhyme
that's
not
necessarily
a poem,
okay?

But
a kiss
always
is

9

Half Rhymes

Like the picture you show Miss Card
Who says, That isn't too bad

Or the scarf you give to Aunt Flower
Who says, That isn't my colour

Or when your best friend's playing catch
And she says, If you like, you can watch

Or the day you thought wouldn't come
When you walk to school on your own

Wind Haiku

The wind shakes the school
Like the beat of a dragon's wing
On a dark night

Commas

I love commas
because they
remind me
of
tadpoles

Change of Position

I had been standing on my teacher's two feet
For some time
When she remarked –
Stand on your own two feet
For once!

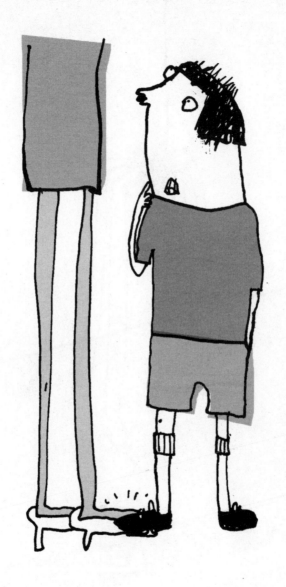

Alone in the Classroom

Crawling across the classroom
Is a black, shiny beetle called Bill

A fat, furry fly called Fred
Sits on the window sill

A thin, hairy spider called Sid
Hangs from the PE shelf

A boy who's been naughty called Me
Sits all by himself

I am staying in at playtime
Just me, myself and I

All alone with my regrets
And a beetle, a spider, a fly

Bad Speller's Acrostic

B other! My spelling

A lways gose rong, I

D on't know why. But

S umtimes it's

P erfict

E speshally if I praktis

L ots and lots

E venchoowally I

R eelly will be abel two spell

Who Lives in the School Pond?

Water boatmen rowing home
Water spiders skip and scurry
Tiny fish dart through the weeds
Pond skaters in a hurry
Dragonflies with whizzing wings
Turquoise bodies catch the light
Worms who live down in the mud
Fat old frogs who hide from sight
It's like a complicated play
I could stay and watch all day

The Water Cycle

A hot day
A glass of cool water

I wonder
How old that water is?

Three minutes old
Poured from the tap?

Or older?

Three hours old
Drawn from the reservoir?

Or older?

Three days
Trapped as condensation
in grey clouds?

Three years
Swirling in the ocean or a great lake
Until the sun turned it to steam
And it rose invisibly up into the sky?

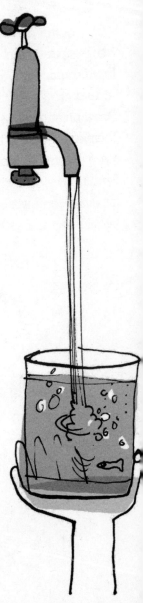

Or maybe three hundred years
Three thousand years
Three million years

Maybe that water
In the glass
Was once a cool refreshing drink
For a brontosaurus
Wandering along the shoreline
Of a prehistoric pool

So drink your glass of water

Enjoy it

And pass it on

More Commas

I love commas,
but my teacher tells me,
that, I, use,
too, many,

Well,
I, don't, agree,

＇

＇

＇

Silent Song

I find
A small, white egg
Under the conker tree
In the corner of the school field

I hold
The small, white egg
In the palm of my hand
And look up into the dark branches

The tree
Is empty and
The small, white egg
Is cold

I think
There is a song
Inside the small, white egg
That we will never hear

Penalty Shot

It was only a kick-about in the park
It was only a bit of fun
It really wasn't your fault, Dad
It could have happened to anyone

You are not as young as you were, Dad
It's a while since you last played the game
And without your Bobby Charlton boots
Well, how can you be the one to blame?

But you can still kick the ball, Dad
That sure was a powerful shot
It was nearly Goal of the Month, Dad
You didn't miss by a lot

The bus driver should have seen it
It was an easy ball to avoid
I don't think the policeman was angry
He was only a trifle annoyed

It was just bad luck that the bus driver swerved
Into the Mayor's Rolls-Royce
With the topspin you cleverly put on the ball
He really had no choice

And when the Rolls smashed into the pet shop
Everyone rallied around
To round up the rabbits and hamsters
And I'm sure that the snake will be found

At least no one was hurt, Dad
So there's no need to be so upset
And on the bright side your penalty shot
Made the front of the Tipton Gazette

Why Me?

I wanted to be Rooney
My pace a scary threat
I wanted to be Gerrard
Precise as you can get

I wanted to be the playmaker
The team's heart and its soul
I didn't want to be the mug
Who hangs about in goal

Travelling

We like to drive
To the motorway bridge
There we sit and watch the traffic
Flow beneath it

We like to drive
Down to the sea
We watch the waves
Sometimes we wave at the ferry
We eat our crisps
You just can't beat it

We like to drive to the station
To watch the trains arrive
Or sometimes to the airport
Where the planes flash silver in the sky
As they leap from the ground

Yes, we are keen travellers
We get around a bit

Mirror Image

I practised
With my guitar
Before the mirror
In my room
Holding the guitar
By the neck
And swinging
Cunning ground strokes
Dazzling serves
Lazy lobs
And thunderous volleys
One day I'll be
The world's greatest
Tennis player

Holiday in Provence

Each step we took
on the dried-out grass
released a dozen grasshoppers –
each step a starting gun
in the jump-every-way-at-once race

Italian Poem

It's five o'clock
We are high in the Umbrian hills
We hear a cuckoo
Somewhere in the mountain oaks
There! See it?
A tiny speck on a distant branch
I reach for the binoculars
But the rogue's gone
Dad says,
You'll just have to wait an hour
For the next one

Old Salt

The grizzled Old Salt says,
Ride round the Bay?
Only a pound, son
It's a lovely day

I once was a pirate
On Captain Kidd's ship
I swung a mean broadsword
I fired from the hip

Then he chuckles and grins,
So, what do you say?
I'm three hundred and thirty
It's my birthday today

Well, he's having me on
He's laughing at me
But I jump in his boat
And we ride out to sea

And he tells me such tales
Of cannons a-singing
And blood on the decks
And cutlasses ringing

Then we're back at the quay
The trip's over so soon
And he slips in my hand
A golden doubloon

Death Cycle Haiku

Rushing down the hill
A bicycle

A beetle
Fails to cross the road

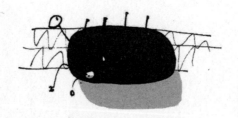

Farewell, Pete

I had a little dinosaur
Nothing would it eat
But a chocolate cupcake
And my best mate, Pete

At school it burst the football
It wasn't fond of sports
It gobbled up the goalposts
and Mr Walton's shorts

It chased my Auntie Emma
You should have heard her shout
But it didn't like my granny
In fact, it spat her out

My Mobile Phone

I love my mobile phone
My mobile phone's called Ben
And when I'm all alone
My mobile phone's my friend

Ben will always ring me
If I'm feeling low
And then Ben starts to sing to me

eee eee eee eee eee eee eee eee
eee eee eee eee eee eee
eee eee eee eee eee eee eee eee
eee eee eee eee eee eee
eee eee eee eee eee eee eee eee
eee eee eee eee eee eee
eee eee eee eee eee eee eee eee
eee eee eee eee eee eee*

And I say, Hello.

*Sung to the tune of 'Supercalifragilisticexpialidocious'

What a Racket

Dad shouts, What a racket
Turn it down, right away
Sounds like cats being strangled
That's not music, no way!

The singer can't sing
She's way out of tune
I've heard better in the market
On a wet afternoon

Where on earth did you get that?
It's worse than bad!
I said, I found it in the attic
In a box marked Dad

Earthquake

I thought there would be sound,
When the earth moved
In stereo, Sensurround!
A rumbling, a crack
An explosion underground

I thought it would be fun,
When the earth moved
Dodging falling chimney pots in slo-mo
We'd run outside and watch
As buildings turned to rubble
Like a picture show

I thought it would be exciting
When the earth moved
Listening to the fire engine's song
A soap opera
An interview with the TV crew
But somehow I'd forgotten
About the dying and the wounded
And the people trapped below

I thought it would be great
To be there when the ground moved
From beneath my feet
But I was wrong

Photograph

A fossil's like a photograph
Developed in the rock
See?
A one-hundred-million-year-old smile

Whoops!

A million little dinosaurs
Having a good time
One fell over a cliff
And then there were
nine hundred and ninety-nine thousand,
nine hundred and ninety-nine

Nine hundred and ninety-nine thousand,
nine hundred and ninety-nine dinosaurs
Having lots of fun
An asteroid hit the Earth
And then there were none

The Owl and the Pussycat

The owl and the pussycat
Went to sea
The owl ate the pussycat
Oh deary me

Hey Diddle Diddle

Hey diddle diddle
The cat and the fiddle
The cow jumped over the bed
The little dog laughed
But not for long
Cos the cow landed right on his head

Peter Piper

(easy version)

Peter Piper chose a large number
Of peppers that had been soaked in vinegar and spices

A large number of peppers
that had been soaked in vinegar and spices
was chosen by Peter Piper

If it is indeed true
That Peter Piper chose a large number
Of peppers that had been soaked in vinegar and spices

Where are they?

Kubla Khant

(Samuel Taylor Coleridge wrote his famous poem after waking from a dream. Halfway through, the postman called and the poem was never finished. This is an up-to-date version.)

In Xanadu did Kubla Khan
Decree a stately pleasure-dome
Where Alph, the sacred river, ran …
Oh blast! There goes my mobile phone

Oak

(after Thomas Hardy)

You were the only oak
For miles around
A giant on the skyline
Home for a thousand creatures
Your trunk three times my span
Your massive roots disturbed the ground

I climbed you once
And sat on your lowest branch
And wished my mates were there to see
I thought that you would outlast time
You were my tree

The workmen came and cut you down
Our friends and neighbours were outraged
It made the papers
And the company was fined
But it was too late
You can't un-fell a tree
I moped around for weeks
Thinking of your winter frame
The greenest green of your spring shoots
The forest of your summer canopy
The day the workmen came

Until one day
I found you on the slope
Between the river and the motorway
A sapling, a mini-you
Not very tall, but vigorous
And reaching up for the sun

Then something in me breathed a sigh
I let your ghost go free
And I got on with my life
You know, school, SATs, maths
Writing poetry

October

(after William Carlos Williams)

leaf
fall
gold

wet
rake
deck

chair
conkers
rolled

beach
ball
get

burst
scars
cold

ache
first
frost

The Things a Dog Has to Do

Clean the kitchen floor lest tiny scraps of food should spoil
the appearance of the tiles
Listen to the wind in case there's a change in the weather
Watch carefully the cat, lest his nerve breaks and he makes a
dash for the window
Guard the window lest the poodle over the road uses
insulting barking
Check, by sniffing, that other dogs have clean bottoms
Check, by sniffing, the four corners of the house for intruders
Check, also by sniffing, the four corners of the garden for the
same

Seek the rotting remnants of dead hedgehogs or other small animals and mark by rolling in them

Watch the toy bone lest it move of its own accord

Remind owner, by subtle means, that it is time for a walk

Remind owner, by less-subtle means, that it is time to eat

Bark loudly for no reason – just for the sheer hell of it and to keep owner on toes

Puzzle over unusual configurations of clouds

Guard the front door lest the postman breaks in to steal a letter

Wonder why the nice man with the tasty bone is coming in through the window and not the door

Mirror Haiku

Look in the mirror
What do you see, pussy cat?
I see a lion.

Hammy Hamster's Great Adventure

He was sitting on Granny's hand
When he noticed the opening
Between the sleeve of her blouse
And her arm
And decided to investigate

Granny said,
Oh
Ha ha
Aah
Eeek
No!
Ah
No
No
Ouch!
Ooooooooh
Whoooh
Hee hee hee
Ah
Ah
No ... no ...
Ouch!
Aaaaaaaaaaaaaaaahhh!

Oooooh
Ha
Heh
Oh
Ooh

And Hammy
Emerging from Granny's left trouser leg
Said,
Hmmm – that was interesting
I think I might try it again

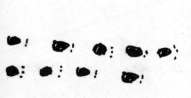

Stone

Hello, old friend
It's good to see you beaming
Bright and fresh faced
Moving through the evening's dreaming

And when I see you newborn
I make a wish
Just like my mother told me to
It's silly, isn't it?
Why would a wish come true?

But when I look up at the clear night sky
And try to count the stars
And feel so overwhelmed
Making a wish is somehow
Not so odd
It's as though you were
A stepping stone to God

Cold Spell

When the Gulf Stream stopped flowing
And the endless snows came in
We packed our memories in fleece and fur
And headed south
Down frosty lanes
Littered with plastic cards
And defunct fridges
Heading for paradise,
The secret fortress
Of our English cousins
In southern Spain

The rumours say
You can walk across the English Channel
On the ice

Crow Haiku

one, two, three, four, five
accumulating darkness
Crow keeps his counsel

The Brown Bear

In the dark wood
In a clearing
Sleeps a brown bear
Dreaming, dreaming

His skin is furless
His paws are clawless
He walks into the city
Lawless, lawless

The moon is hidden
The clouds are weeping
A princess slumbers
Sleeping, sleeping

The thief creeps through
The royal bedroom
And steals her ruby
A priceless heirloom

The ruby glows
With fire and lightning
A spell is cast
So frightening, frightening

The thief grows fur
His body thickens
His hands grow claws
He sickens, sickens

Beneath the black sky
Thunder rumbles
Into the dark wood
He stumbles, stumbles

For in the ruby,
Gleaming, gleaming
A wizard's mind
Is scheming, scheming

Now, in the dark wood
In a clearing
Sleeps a brown bear
Dreaming, dreaming

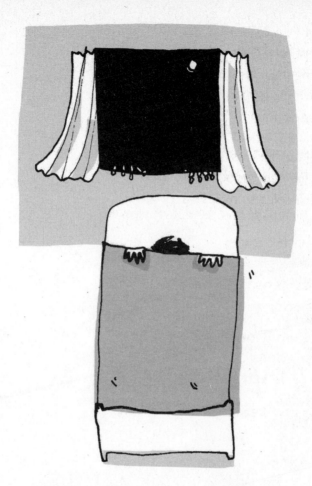

The Ghostly Visitor

I wake up in the night
In a pool of blue moonlight
The curtains are swaying
But there is no wind
The night is still and silent

Silent
Except for the clock
Ticking the minutes past midnight
And in the garden I hear
An eerie sound

An eerie sound
Like bones clicking
Or a body
Dragging itself over the autumn leaves
On the lawn
The sound of a rasping breath
Far away

Far away
But growing louder
Getting closer
The rustle of branch against the wall
Or a claw
Scrabbling

Scrabbling
Beneath my window
Climbing
Trying to gain a purchase on the brick
I am frozen in my bed
Too scared to get up
And turn on the light
I lie still, listening
Until at last the sound recedes
Leaving my garden

Leaving my garden
But clearly heading
In the direction of
Your house

Your house ...

A Poem's Plea

I'm a lonely little poem
I want to be recited
Not just sit in a book
I want to be excited

To be a poem chosen
Be read upon the stage
Not hidden in the darkness
Just words upon a page

Yes, I'm a little poem
And I want to be a star
Now you're going to turn the page I'm on …

Admit it …

Yes, you are …

Nineteen Things to Do
in Winter

Find the sledge at the back of the garage
    Grease the runners and paint it red
Watch the weather report for news of snow
Snuggle up in bed and read a book
    that's as long as a long winter night
Listen to the wind moan

Keep an eye on the sky for snow clouds on the horizon
Draw rude faces on steamed-up windows
Go to football. Watch the Gunners. Groan and cheer
Rescue fish in frozen ponds
    and old ladies at the bottom of icy hills
Drop an icicle down your sister's tights
Warm cold knees and icy bottom around roaring fire
Check the sky for snow
Fit sledge with seats made from cushions of armchair in front
    room
Make balls of fat and birdseed to feed the blue tits
Be sympathetic when Dad fuses the lights
Ring the meteorological office and ask when it's going to
    snow
Paint go-faster stripes on sledge
Say to Mum, I've no idea where the armchair cushions have
    gone
Dream of green trees and buzzing bees and summer seas
Wonder why it hasn't snowed again this year

Protection

I've got woollen underpants
By Jove, I'm glad I've got 'em
Cos when you toboggan and slide in the snow
You can get a very cold bottom

She is

She's a fragile ghost
She's a leaning oak
She's the scruffy trainers and the latest trend
She's burnt toast and a cold Coke
She's a waterlogged moon and the joy of pretend
She's an explosion of shimmering stars
She's the find of lost, the heal of mend
She's the giggling stream
She's a midnight feast
She's the waterfall hidden at the rainbow's end
She's a map of pathways, secret and strange
On a long road with no turning she's the first bend
She's a white starfish on a sunburnt beach
She's each of these things
She's my best friend

Liverpool Cathedral

It's like standing in God's waiting room
Gazing up at an indoors sky
Peering at the shadows high above
Hoping to glimpse a soul
My thoughts
Adrift in that universe
Of smooth brown Woolton sandstone

I feel like a fish
Trying to grab a strand
Of weed
That's floating on the sea's surface
With hands I do not possess

I wonder
Do fish
Believe we can walk on water?

Christmas Morning

Last year
On Christmas morning
We got up really early
And took the dog for a walk
Across the Downs

It wasn't snowing
But the hills were white with frost
And our breath froze
In the air

Judy rushed around like a crazy thing
As though Christmas
Meant something special to her

The sheep huddled together
Looking tired
As if they'd been up all night
Watching the stars

We stood at the highest point
And thought about what Christmas means
And looked over the white hills
And looked up at the blue sky

And the hills seemed
To go on forever
And the sky had no bounds
And you could imagine
A world at peace

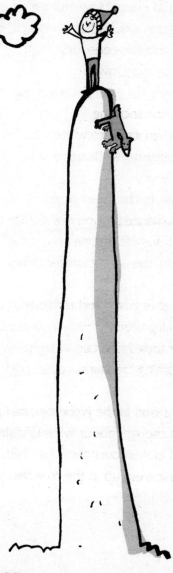

Frequently Asked Questions

Why don't poems always rhyme?
Because poems love making a fuss
They don't like sitting quietly
Although this one does

Where do you get your ideas from?
They come to me in the night
I keep an ideas trap by my bed
And gloves – in case they bite

What is the best poem you ever wrote?
Why Otters Don't Wear Socks
But it was stolen one day and sold on eBay
By a furtive and fraudulent fox

What is your favourite word?
I like crunchy and fizzle and toast
And carpet sure takes some beating
But I think I love loving the most

Why was poet your chosen profession?
At rounding up words I was skilled

If you weren't a poet, what would you be?
Unhappy, unhinged, unfulfilled

What advice can you give to young poets?

If want to succeed, read, read, read
Read, read, read, read, read, read
Read, read, read, read, read, read
Read, read, read, read, read, read
Read and read

(And read! Did I mention that?)

Mum's Grave

It's in a quiet and peaceful spot, I guess
It's made of marble
There are trees, dead leaves and grass

And by the headstone is a wooden letter box
Where we can post our memories
I don't use it a lot
I mainly say a prayer
And let it rise into the cloudy sky
Above Mum's grave
Because she's not down there

Mum's grave is just a line
That's written underneath the word Goodbye

What's the Point?

How rare
to find a poem
ending
with an empty
stop。

Freedom

Below me you are fast asleep
But I am out of sight
As I crawl across your ceiling
A black shape in the night

I am heading for the window
Where the moon lights up the sky
No more a small, cramped tank of glass
My eight arms wave
So long
Farewell
Aloha
Ciao
Adieu
Au revoir
Toodle pip

Goodbye

The Monster That Ate The Universe

Poems by Roger Stevens

A glorious collection of poems from the
wonderful Roger Stevens, in which he covers
subjects as varied as monsters, Halloween, snow,
dinosaurs, love, science, parents who dance and
chicken school.

chicken School

Period one – simple clucking

Period two – more clucking

Period three – clucking with attitude

Period four – clucking with indecision

Period five – pecking in dirt

Period six – pecking in gravel

Period seven – rhythmic and jerky neck movements

Period eight – clucking (revision)

HOW TO SURVIVE SCHOOL

Poems chosen by

David Harmer

**Forget textbooks or calculators, HERE is the essential
item you need to survive school!**

Discover the best way to deal with every school occasion.
Learn how to outwit the dinner lady and befriend the care-
taker, how to divert attention from yourself and appear to
be paying attention and how to win the best part in the
school play.

My Best Subject

I'm no good at history, rubbish at maths
And geography, and all the rest;
But at blackmailing teachers I'm really quite good,
So I always do well in the tests.

Rob Falconer

A selected list of poetry titles available from Macmillan Children's Books

The prices shown below are correct at the time of going to press. However, Macmillan Publishers reserves the right to show new retail prices on covers, which may differ from those previously advertised.